Date: 02/01/12

J 639.395 STE
Stevens, Kathryn,
Lizards /

PET CARE FOR KIDS

LIZARDS

BY KATHRYN STEVENS

The Child's World

Published by The Child's World®
1980 Lookout Drive • Mankato, MN 56003-1705
800-599-READ • www.childsworld.com

Acknowledgments
The Child's World®: Mary Berendes, Publishing Director
The Design Lab: Kathleen Petelinsek, Design and Page Production

Photo Credits: 123RF.com/ssilver: 18; fStop/Alamy: 17; iStockphoto.
com/ChoiceGraphX: 13; iStockphoto.com/Eric Isselée: front
cover, back cover, 1, 3, 4, 22 (dragon, chameleon, geckoes), 6, 21;
iStockphoto.com/Gabriela Schaufelberger: 7; iStockphoto.com/
Jim White: front cover, 1, 24 (anole); iStockphoto.com/Josiah
Garber: 11; iStockphoto.com/Noam Armonn: 12 (chameleon);
iStockphoto.com/Oktay Ortakcioglu: 12, 20 (rock); iStockphoto.com/
Tomasz Zachariasz: front cover, back cover, 1, 3, 14, 20 (crickets);
iStockphoto.com/Windzepher: 19; John Anderson/dreamstime.com:
5; Juniors Bildarchiv/Alamy: 9; PhotoDisc: 3 (gecko), 10; Podius/
dreamstime.com: front cover, back cover, 3, 8, 20 (tank); Teresa
Kenney/dreamstime.com: 15; Thomas Perkins/dreamstime.com: 16

Library of Congress Cataloging-in-Publication Data
Stevens, Kathryn, 1954–
  Lizards / by Kathryn Stevens.
    p. cm. — (Pet care for kids)
  Includes index.
  ISBN 978-1-60253-185-7 (library bound : alk. paper)
  1. Lizards as pets—Juvenile literature. I. Title. II. Series.
  SF459.L5S89 2009
  639.3'95—dc22   2008040806

Published in the United States of America
Mankato, Minnesota
March, 2010
PA02047

NOTE TO PARENTS AND EDUCATORS

The Pet Care for Kids series is written for children who want to be part of the pet experience but are too young to be in charge of pets themselves. These books are intended to provide a kid-friendly supplement to more detailed information adults need to know about choosing and caring for different types of pets. They can help youngsters learn how to live happily with the animals in their lives, and, with adults' help and supervision, grow into responsible animal caretakers later on.

PET CARE FOR KIDS

CONTENTS

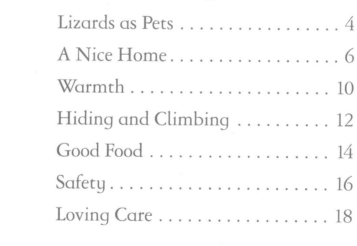

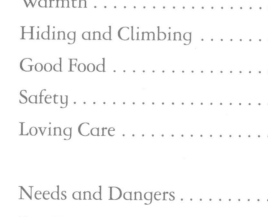

LIZARDS AS PETS

Lizards are great animals. Many people think having a pet lizard would be fun. But they should learn about lizards first. Lizards need special care and handling. They can live for 10 or 15 years—or even longer! Getting a lizard is a big decision.

▶ This baby green iguana is cute. But he will grow to 6 feet (nearly 2 meters) long! Most people cannot take care of such a big lizard.

◀ Leopard geckos are only about 8 inches (20 centimeters) long. Many people keep them as pets. But geckos and other lizards should never be taken from the wild.

A NICE HOME

Wild lizards live in lots of different places. Some live in warm, dry areas. Others live in places that are **moist** or even wet. Pet lizards' homes should feel like their wild homes. They should have the right warmth and moisture. But the homes should also be easy to clean.

▶ Pet chameleons (kuh-MEE-lee-unz) need homes like those in the wild. They must have lots of branches and leaves to climb on.

◀ This chameleon is holding on with its tail as well as its feet!

Most pet lizards live in clear tanks. The tanks are like **aquariums** used for keeping fish. Some lizards like to live alone. Others do not mind living together. A lizard's tank should have plenty of room. Different kinds of lizards need different-sized tanks.

This Australian bearded dragon has a nice home. It has a warm light, a water dish, and places to climb and hide.

Getting the right-sized tank is important!

WARMTH

Lizards need outside heat to warm their bodies. Wild lizards warm up in the sun. They cool off in the shade. Pet lizards need the right warmth, too. A light or heater warms one part of the tank. Other parts stay cooler. The lizard chooses where it wants to be.

▶ This iguana is warming itself under the lamp in its cage.

▼ Bearded dragons are active during the day and sleep at night. Some kinds of lizards are active at night instead.

HIDING AND CLIMBING

Wild lizards are good at hiding. Hiding helps them stay alive. Pet lizards like to hide, too. Each lizard needs at least one hiding place. Many lizards climb really well, too. Some like to climb a lot. Taller tanks have more room for climbing.

▶ This anole (uh-NOH-lee) is hiding between some leaves in its cage.

▼ Many lizards like to hide under rocks.

◀ Green chameleons like this one are good climbers.

GOOD FOOD

Different kinds of lizards need different kinds of foods. People need to learn which foods their lizards need. Some lizards eat bugs. Pet stores sell crickets for these lizards to eat. Other lizards eat fruits and vegetables.

▶ This bearded dragon is eating lettuce.

◀ Pet stores sell special foods or powders for crickets. They make the crickets healthier for lizards to eat.

SAFETY

Many lizards carry germs that can make people sick. People need to wash up after handling a lizard. The lizard's tank must be kept clean, too. Good food and clean homes help lizards stay healthy. But sometimes lizards need to visit animal doctors, or **vets**.

▶ An adult is in charge of this bearded dragon's care. She is helping children handle the lizard safely.

◀ Cleaning up after handling a lizard is important. Very young children should not handle lizards at all.

LOVING CARE

Lizards are not the easiest pets to care for. But they are fun and interesting. Some people enjoy learning all about lizards. They enjoy taking care of these animals. They can do a good job keeping lizards as pets.

▸ This boy loves his pet leopard gecko. Leopard geckos can live for 20 years or more.

◂ Anoles like this one can live for about 5 years.

NEEDS:

* a clean, roomy tank
* the right warmth and moisture
* warmer and cooler places
* clean water
* the right foods
* places to hide
* sunlight or special lights

DANGERS:

* getting too hot or too cold
* getting too wet or too dry
* a dirty aquarium
* no hiding place
* the wrong foods
* rough handling
* other animals
* getting loose

COLOR:
Some lizards can change color!

SCALES:
Lizards are not slimy. Their bodies are covered with hard, smooth scales.

SWIMMING:
Some lizards swim very well.

JAWS:
All lizards can bite.

FEET:
Some lizards have toes that can stick to smooth walls.

TAILS:
Some lizards' tails drop off if something grabs them!

CLAWS:
Lizards have claws on their feet.

GLOSSARY

aquariums (*uh-KWAYR-ee-ums*) Aquariums are clear tanks where animals can live.

moist (*MOYST*) Something that is moist has just a little water in it.

vets (*VETS*) Vets are doctors who take care of animals. Vet is short for "veterinarian" (*vet-rih-NAYR-ee-un*).

TO FIND OUT MORE

Books:

Heathcote, Peter. *Lizards*. Chicago, IL: Heinemann Library, 2004.

Little, Jean, and Jennifer Plecas (illustrator). *Emma's Strange Pet*. New York: HarperCollins, 2003.

Schafer, Susan. *Lizards*. New York: Benchmark Books/Marshall Cavendish, 2001.

Waters, Jo. *The Wild Side of Pet Lizards*. Chicago, IL: Raintree, 2005.

Video/DVD:

Paws, Claws, Feathers & Fins: A Kid's Guide to Happy, Healthy Pets. Goldhil Learning Series (Video 1993, DVD 2005).

Web Sites:

Visit our Web page for lots of links about pet care:
http://www.childsworld.com/links

Note to parents, teachers, and librarians: We routinely verify our Web links to make sure they are safe, active sites—so encourage your readers to check them out!

INDEX

ABOUT THE AUTHOR

Kathryn Stevens has authored and edited many books for young readers, including books on animals ranging from grizzly bears to fleas. She's a lifelong pet-lover and currently cares for a big, huggable pet-therapy dog named Fudge.